Ernest H. Andrae

A Guide to the Cultivation of the Grape-Vine in Texas, and

Instructions for Wine-Making

Ernest H. Andrae

A Guide to the Cultivation of the Grape-Vine in Texas, and Instructions for Wine-Making

ISBN/EAN: 9783337329068

Printed in Europe, USA, Canada, Australia, Japan

Cover: Foto ©Lupo / pixelio.de

More available books at **www.hansebooks.com**

A GUIDE TO THE

CULTIVATION

—OF THE—

GRAPE-VINE

IN TEXAS,

—AND—

Instructions for Wine-Making,

—BY—

E. H. ANDRAE.

TEXAS FARM AND RANCH PUBLISHING CO., Publishers,

DALLAS, TEXAS.

To the Reader.

Considering the immense advantages Texas offers for wine culture, it is surprising that this noble and profitable branch of agriculture so far, comparatively speaking, has found only a small number of followers.

Presuming that the cause for this lack of patronage of ample and apparent natural benefits is only more or less the want of knowledge of a proper *modus operandi*, the author has taken the liberty to compile a small handbook that would place within the reach of everybody the necessary instruction for a successful cultivation of the grape vine, with some directions for fermenting the juice.

No claim to originality is made, but a careful selection from the best writings on the subject, and the practical opinions of some of the most successful grape-growers in Texas, are condensed into the best rudimentary instruction possible in this neglected field of labor.

Due credit is given to respective authors copied.

As for the profits in wine culture, all figures have been left out, but the truth of the following may safely be vouched for:

"That the vineyard will pay for all the labor bestowed on it, but it can not be expected to pay for what it does not receive," which is more than can be said of other parts of husbandry.

With fair profits the culture of the grape-vine furnishes as noble and dignified an employment as there is found in the land, with a fair prospect also of forming in time the only solution of the temperance question, as wine so far is the only form of alcoholic beverages that satisfies the craving for an intoxicant, with none of the maddening, crime-begetting characteristics of other alcoholic drinks.

To any man who possibly might have religious scruples as to fermenting the juice of the grape, I recommend Proverbs, Chap. 31, 6–7, which part of the scripture seems hardly to be known, even by would-be Theologians.

With the sincere wish that this book may be one step towards *sitting under your own vine and fig tree,* and especially to my former "brethren in good standing" this book is respectfully introduced.

The Author.

CONTENTS.

***

FIRST PART.

***

SECOND PART.

THE GRAPE VINE.

(*VITIS*.)

There are more than 1500 different varieties of the grape vine in cultivation. However accurate and minute a description be of one kind, it would still be exceedingly difficult for a novice to recognize a variety from a mere portraiture of its general appearance and characteristics by words. Besides, it would be almost impossible to give a passable description in a small volume like the present, of even the commoner kinds, as a description should include :

1. The name, synonyms, origin, home and place of cultivation.

2. History and literature, with illustrations.

3. The vine, its characteristics, vigor of growth, fertility, hardness and hardiness.

4. Wood, if heavy or light, long or short jointed, color of wood, character of the eye or bud.

5. Shoots, if pushing early or late, smooth or hairy.

6. Leaves, foliage, its size, shape, sinuosity, (lobed) upper and lower surface, if smooth, glossy, hairy or wooly.

7. Petiole, stem of the leaf, if long, short, hairy, smooth, green or red.

8. Leaf-fall, if early or late, change of color to yellow or red.

9. Bunch, size and shape, shouldered or not, compact or loose.

10. Stem, peduncles and tendrils, if long or short, smooth or warty, intermittent or continuous.

11. Berries, size, shape, skin, color, pulp or flesh, taste and use, if for table or wine, or both, with keeping quality.

12. Period of ripening, if early, medium, late, etc.

For the reasons given above, a list only of the chief and original varieties is given here to serve as the first step in ampelography, as the description of grape vines is called, for the amateur grape grower.

THE EUROPEAN VARIETIES.
(VITIS VINIFERA.)

Under this name are known several hundred of European (and part Asiatic) varieties. It is this sort that has been the delight of man from immemorial time, being mentioned repeatedly in Scripture. Grows only successfully in Europe, California, Arizona, New Mexico and, hybridized with American varieties, in Texas. Although repeatedly introduced in other States east of the Rocky Mountains, have never there been really a success, and after living a few years have invariably succumbed to the attacks of the root louse (*phylloxera*). This insect, originally a native of America, is now devastating the vineyards of Europe, where it has been accidentally introduced, and would evidently there destroy all the vines were it not for the American varieties, which, by their vigorous growth or other special qualities, effectually resist the attacks of this insect, and are for this reason extensively imported into France and other European countries to graft upon. There are two kinds of *phylloxera*—the root louse, attached to the ends of the rootlets of the vine, and the gall louse, inhabiting the galls or warts sometimes found underneath the leaf. Both are about 1-25 inch long, the former of a dull brown and the latter of dull orange color. During the first year of the attacks of the root louse the vine seems scarcely affected, but the ends of the rootlets soon swell up in consequence of the attack and begin to rot, when the root louse will leave them for other roots, until the vine is dead. The successive dying of the vine by the root louse resembles very much the cotton blight in Texas. So far, no remedy has been found to stop the ravages of the pest, except irrigation, where practicable, for five or six weeks, and grafting on American stocks.

The *Vinifera* vine, which unfortunately is so sadly exposed to the *phylloxera pest*, may briefly be described as follows :

Leaves, shining, five to seven lobed, pointed and sharply toothed, cottony only when very young; berries, mostly large and of delicious taste; seeds, mostly notched at the upper end, beak elongated. In some varieties the leaves and branchlets are hairy or downy when young. Some kinds seem to correspond in appearance to some of the American varieties, but are otherwise different in characteristics.

THE AMERICAN VARIETIES,

Of which are understood only those with edible berries, are still found growing wild, although numerous varieties have been cultivated for centuries. The American grape vine has, since the discovery of its *phylloxera* resisting quality, become quite an important article in those countries where the *Vinifera* vines are extensively cultivated, and are exported continually to Europe to be used as grafting stocks. The following are about the chief varieties, or family groups:

1. **Vitis Labrusca,** (Linn), or Fox Grape of the North, originally a native of the Alleghany mountains, on the eastern slope to the sea coast—the original of the Catawba and Isabella. Leaves large, and these and young shoots very cottony, even the adult leaves retaining their cottony wool underneath the lobes, separated by roundish sinuses; continuous tendrils; large berries in large bunches with a foxy taste. Grows well on granitic soil. More a table variety than a wine grape.

2. **Vitis Candicans.** (Engelmann.) [*Vitis Mustangensis, Buckley.*] The well known Mustang Grape of Texas. Toothless, many-lobed leaves, white, cottony on the underside; large berries of various colors—green, claret and bluish black.

3. **Vitis Monticola.** (Buckley), or Little Mountain Grape, of Southwestern Texas. Usually a small, bushy vine with intermittent tendrils; three-lobed, broad-toothed leaves; bunches of fruit compact and short, berries middle-sized, green and palatable. Easily propagated from cuttings. *Vitis Arizonica* (Engelmann) in Arizona and New Mexico is closely related to this.

4. **Vitis Aestivalis.** (Michaux.) The Summer Grape, common throughout the Middle and Southern States. Usually found on uplands and in dry, open woods or thickets. Forked, intermittent tendrils; leaves large, three to five deeply lobed, with rounded sinuses and short, broad teeth; berries middle-sized, sometimes large and black, in compact, often cylindrical, bunches. It is pre-emin] tly *the wine grape* this side of the Rocky Mountains, the juice containing a larger percentage of sugar than any other American

kind. It is also one of the most variable varieties and hard
to propagate by cuttings, while slips will grow off well.
Well known varieties of the *Aestivalis* are the Cunningham,
Herbemont and Lenoir. The latter is also called Texas
Black Spanish. *Vitis Lincecumi*, or Postoak Grape of
Texas, is counted among this variety. This is a more
bushy than climbing vine, with large berries, leaves three to
five lobed and coated with a thick, rusty down.

5. **Vitis Cinera.** (Engelmann.) Closely allied to *Aestivalis*.
Found in bottom lands and along banks of lakes in the
Mississippi Valley and Texas, with gray-downy three-
lobed leaves, small black berries, with pleasant acid taste,
until frost sweetens them.

6. **Vitis Cordifolia.** (Michaux.) Winter or Frost Grape, growing in the Middle States and Texas. Leaves large, three
to four inches wide, not lobed, or slightly three-lobed,
small, shining black berries, with a disagreeable strong
flavor, only edible after frost. Will not grow from cuttings.

7. **Vitis Riparia.** (Michaux.) Grape Vine of the River Bank,
growing in almost all the States between Canada and
Texas. Favors in appearance the *Cordifolia*. Leaves three-
lobed, with sharp teeth of light green, glabrous (smooth)
and often hairy below; small black berries in small, compact bunches. Now extensively used in France. Grows
easily from cuttings. Although the berries are very juicy,
the wine is generally excessively acid, but sometimes im-
proves with age.

8. **Vitis Rupestris,** (Scheele), or Land Grape of Missouri, Sugar
Grape of Texas. A native of the hilly country west of the
Mississippi. Grows easily from cuttings. Leaves rather
small (three inches wide), of very pale green color, rarely
lobed, with broad, coarse teeth; small, sweet berries in very
small bunches. Valuable grafting stock, and considered
well adapted to graft *Vinifera* varieties upon.

9. **Vitis Rotundifolia.** (Michaux.) [*Vitis Vulpina, Linn.*] Mus-
cadine, Bullace, or Fox Grape of the South, the original of
the Scuppernong. Leaves rather small, heart-shaped, sel-
dom or slightly lobed, glossy and mostly smooth on both
sides, coarse and broad toothed ; clusters small, fruit large
(½ to ¾ inch in diameter), purple, thick-skinned, musky or

pleasant flavored, ripe in early autumn. Cannot be grown from cuttings, and is also unfit for grafting purposes on account of the hardness of the wood and different construction of the bark. Introduced in Texas at various times, it has always so far proved a failure.

Either through the agencies of insects, birds or the efforts and skill of man, or sometimes accidentally, the above varieties have been hybridized, or crossed, to an enormous extent, and it is extremely difficult, even for the experienced botanist, to tell by appearance to which family the grape belongs. Some nurserymen classify many as a pure variety, while botanists and others pronounce them hybrids. An instance of this is the Delaware, commonly believed to be a pure *Labrusca,* while others, of good authority, consider it a cross between *Vinifera* and *Labrusca,* or *Riparia* and *Vinifera.* Another is the Taylor-Bulitt, generally classified as *Riparia,* when some assert it is a natural hybrid between *Labrusca* and *Riparia.* The seeds of the different varieties furnish perhaps the best guide to classification, as also would a thorough illustration of the structures of the canes, but reference must be had to more comprehensive works on the subject by those seeking to perfect themselves in that part of grape lore.

The above named groups may also be divided into Northern and Southern varieties, as, for instance, a *Labrusca* vine growing in the north may be different from one growing farther south, at least in the kind of wine made from the juice, although both vines may be pure *Labruscas.* The same may be said of *Riparia, Aestivalis, Rupestris* and *Vulpina.* The *Aestivalis,* though, may be said to be almost exclusively a Southern, and especially a Texas, vine, since none of its varieties will ripen without hothouse protection north of the parallel of 40 degrees, and in Texas, whether wild or cultivated, seem to succeed better than any other.

For unaccountable reasons, the *Aestivalis* vine cannot boast of as many varieties as others, although the berries are generally juicy and aromatic when of the smaller sorts, and by crossing with other kinds of larger fruit, some valuable varieties might have been obtained, the more so as the *Aestivalis* of Texas are generally considered free of rot.

The wood of the true *Aestivalis* is very solid and hard, with small pith and firm outer bark, so that it is almost impossible to grow from cuttings, while making valuable grafting stocks.

We may state here that experiments with artificial cross-fertilizing (hybridizing) the native American with the European (*Vinifera*) kinds has so far been unsatisfactory ; at least, the vines, while showing superior quality of fruit, did not show the hardiness and *phylloxera* resisting quality necessary this side of the Rocky Mountains. The few varieties with *Vinifera* blood in them possess such in a very limited degree, generally about one-fourth.

It is also not advisable for the average grape grower to try experiments in crossing on an extended scale, but to leave this risky part of grape culture to nurserymen rather, as they are generally better fitted and more experienced.

Although grape vines are generally vigorous growers, they are all subject to particular climatic conditions, and it is for this reason that some vines only are suited to particular localities.

OF THE VINES THAT HAVE STOOD THE TEST
IN TEXAS,

and have been cultivated in various localities for a number of years, and may be relied upon, are the following :

AGAWAM.—A hybrid (most likely *Labr.* and some *Vinifera*), with brownish maroon colored, very large, globular berries, thick skin, soft pulp, sweet and aromatic flavor. Ripens soon after the Concord, making an early table grape rather than wine grape.

BLACK JULY, or DEVEREUX.—Belonging to the same class as the Herbemont and Cunningham [*Aest.*]. A Southern grape, black and small, making a fine wine, especially if made into white wine. Ripening late and almost exclusively a wine grape.

BLACK EAGLE.—A hybrid [*Labr.* and *Vinifera*], a fine early table grape. Large, black berries. By some considered the best all-around grape of any.

BLACK SPANISH, or LENOIR, EL PASO, BURGUNDY, JACK or JACQUES.— A Southern grape of the Herbemont class. [*Aest.*] Ripens late. Small black berries, making an excellent alcoholic red wine. An almost typical Texas variety.

BRIGHTON —[Hybrid between *Labr.* and some other.] An early

table grape, ripening a month earlier than Catawba, large, round berries, almost black when ripe.

CATAWBA.—[*Labr.*] Has been for years a standard grape, both for wine and table use, ripening rather late, round, red berries, rather large.

CONCORD.—[*Labr.*] Both table and wine grape, ripening tolerably early. Large, black berries, making a light red wine.

DELAWARE.—[Hybrid, most likely *Labr.* and some *Vinifera.*] An early table and wine grape. Small berries of beautiful light red, making a good wine.

DUCHESS.—[Hybrid.] Both table and wine grape. A cross of Concord and Delaware. Berries medium sized, of pale, greenish yellow when ripe.

GOETHE.—[Hybrid of *Labr.* and *Vinifera*] A late grape, growing splendidly in sandy land, both for table use and for wine. The only hybrid where the fruit resembles the European vine and the stock keeps the native vigor. Berries very large, of yellowish green color, making a splendid wine. Should not be allowed to over bear itself, which would ruin its productiveness for years, if not for always.

HARTFORD PROLIFIC.—[*Labr*] A very early market grape, ripening about ten days earlier than the Concord. Is not considered a good wine grape. Berries round, black and medium sized.

HERBEMONT —[*Æst.*] A late wine and table grape, of excellent qualities, flourishing especially in Texas. Small black, highly-flavored berries. The pure juice, pressed without previously mashing the grape, makes a delicate white wine. If fermented on the husks about forty-eight hours, making a fine pale red wine.

PETER WYLIE.—[Hybrid of Halifax, Delaware and *Vinifera.*] A table grape, ripening neither early nor late, medium-sized berries of a golden yellow when ripe.

TRIUMPH.— [Hybrid of *Labrusca* and others.] A magnificent table grape, ripening late. Very large berries of pale green or golden yellow.

The EARLY HAMBURG, MUSCATEL and others have also been doing well in some parts of the State. Some mildew and rot are liable to appear in any locality in extraordinary wet seasons, and there may be many other valuable varieties suited to one part of the State and less so in another.

Too great a variety of grapes in the vineyard is not always desirable, especially where it is intended to make wine, as different varieties mean also different periods of ripening, which may happen at unsuitable times, and interfere with making wine materially. Late varieties generally make the best wine.

LAYERS AND CUTTINGS.

The grape vine may be reproduced or propagated by its seed, and there may be circumstances where this would be not only desirable, but necessary. But as the cultivated varieties, from which the amateur grape grower most likely would wish to propagate, are more or less hybrids, the seeds from such are not likely to reproduce the hybridized variety, but rather will produce plants with the characteristics of the original parent plants. Besides, by planting the seeds, frequently, only male plants will sprout, which never would bear fruit. The wild grapes reproduce themselves from the seed constantly, and the seedlings do not materially differ from the parent vine. But it is rarely done, and the only propagating practiced now is by *layering* and *cutting*, either one of which will exactly reproduce the parent vine.

Layers may be obtained as follows, both from cultivated and wild varieties :

In the summer bend a vine of last season's growth down to the ground, pegging it there if necessary. Cut it almost in two where it touches the earth and cover the cut part several inches with dirt, leaving the ends above the ground. When well rooted, the layer thus obtained will be ready to sever from the stock and may be transplanted. Vines more than one year old should not be layered.

Considering the amount of wild vines bearing fruit in Texas, which, if they would not do for making into wine, would all make excellent grafting stocks for other choice varieties, the reader will observe what splendid opportunities are offered him to start a vineyard with hardly any cost but his labor.

Care should be taken in propagating by layers and cuttings that the vine is of a fruit bearing variety, and that its berries are edible.

The art and manner of obtaining and planting *Cuttings* may be understood best by the following, from "Orchard and Garden":

"Although the best time for making cuttings is in the fall, as soon as the wood has fully ripened, yet it may be done in the early winter months. In making the cuttings, if the variety is scarce, two-eyed cuttings are made, cutting above and below a bud, and thus leaving one at the top and the base, but three-eyed cuttings, consisting of two joints of wood, are much better and make much stronger vines. Where the variety is particularly rare, it is often propagated by what is known as single eyes; that is, each eye is cut with about one inch of wood above and below it; but this mode is more difficult, and is practiced chiefly by professional men.

"The cuttings when made should be tied into small bundles and buried in the earth, selecting a spot where the water does not stand and raising a small mound over them to shed the water. In spring they are taken up and set where they are to grow. In planting, the cuttings are inserted in the ground so that only the bud and an inch or so of wood is above the surface, and it is important the soil should be packed tightly around them, so as to completely exclude the air.

"We do not think it injures cuttings to be made when the wood is frozen, as claimed by some, nor does it injure the vine to prune it whilst the wood is frozen if it is not broken or injured in bending the vine."

The first year is considered the best time for transplanting the young vines. Vines more than two years old should not be transplanted. Growing vines from green cuttings and unhealthy wood should be avoided.

GRAFTING.

This is a method of propagating and improving the vine, which any farmer ought to be acquainted with, as it is a valuable part of his profession, and is by no means as difficult an operation as most people are inclined to suppose.

Grafting is practiced now in Europe on an enormous scale, and forms there the only means of saving the vineyards from utter destruction by the root louse (*phylloxera*), for which purpose the American grape vines are raised there from the seed or imported directly, on which stocks the valuable *Vinifera* are grafted afterwards.

It is a curious fact, though, that the grafting of the *Vinifera* on American stocks has not been as successful in America as in Europe, which fact may after all be due only to climatic conditions, and it may still be possible to grow the best *Vinifera* on American roots in favored localities east of the Rocky Mountains, especially in Texas.

The stock should be strong and healthy. It is not necessary that it should be of the same variety.

The scion should be from a healthy, short-jointed cane of last summer's growth, about the thickness of a lead pencil. Scions are generally cut in the fall, before the hard freezing weather sets in, and kept in a cool place in damp moss, sand or sawdust until grafting time.

This is any time in fall, after the falling of the leaves, and before the rising of the sap in spring. It may also be done after the sap has risen, but must then be delayed until the flow of sap has somewhat subsided, as cutting of the vine while the sap is rising will produce profuse "bleeding" and thereby injure the stock. February and March generally furnish a good opportunity. It may also be done later, in midsummer, with the scions of the same season's growth.

CLEFT GRAFTING

Is perhaps the simplest method, and is generally done under ground, and not, as with fruit trees, above it. It is practiced rather on larger stocks—from one-half inch to three inches in diameter—but can be used also efficiently on smaller ones.

Clear away the soil around the stock to the depth of about three to four inches; clean off the stock well; then with a fine-toothed saw or sharp knife cut the vine off horizontally about level with the surface of the ground, or sometimes a little lower. Split the stock with a chisel, wedge, hatchet or other sharp instrument without mutilating it. The cleft to run down the stock about one and a half or two inches. Hold open the cleft by inserting a thinner wedge into it. Then with a very sharp knife cut two scions to fit the cleft, to more or less of a long wedge, leaving two eyes.

Insert the scions so that the bark of both stock and scion fit as nearly perfectly as possible; then withdraw your centre wedge and the stock will hold the scions firmly. Wind around the graft some coarse string or yarn, but not so that it will cut into the bark, and cover the cuts with a grafting clay, made out of one part fresh cow dung and four parts soft clay. Do not use grafting wax, as it is more likely to injure than to benefit.

Fill up around the stock with dirt, so that only the upper bud of the scion is above ground.

When it is intended to graft a *Vinifera* [European] variety on an American stock, care should be taken that the scion itself does not take root, as the *phyllovera* [root louse]—almost about anywhere—will soon attack such roots and kill the scion. Less dirt is therefore generally put on such a graft, and all sprouting roots promptly pinched off.

With other grafts than *Vinifera*, root-making should be rather encouraged, though, as it would decidedly assist the young graft in growing off.

The cleft graft for thick stocks may also be used for one scion only, by splitting the stock down on one side about half way across and cutting the scion with the outer bark side thicker so as to form a wedge towards the centre of the stock, as well as downward.

The cleft graft as above described is also of decided advantage on smaller stocks, especially when both sides of the bark can be brought in contact with each other.

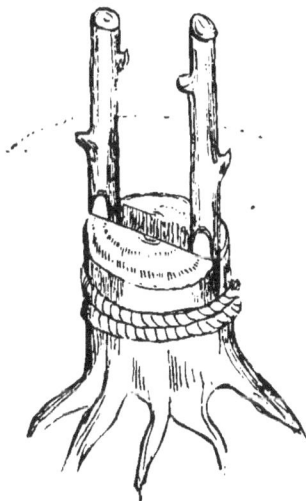

Cleft Graft for thick stocks.   Cleft Graft for small stocks.

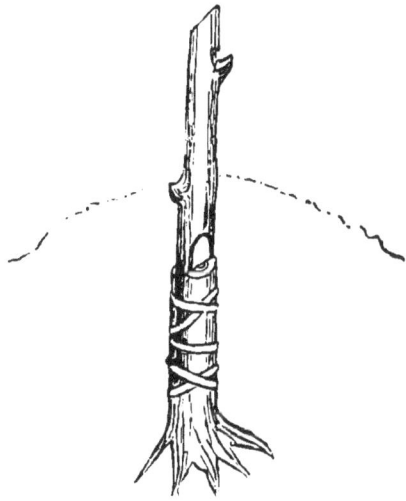

Another method for small stocks or grafting cuttings upon cuttings, is the whip graft, or Champin graft, so named after a Frenchman, Champin, who made considerable improvement in it.

Either with pruning shears or a very sharp knife, cut off the top as close as possible below an eye. Clean off all grit, as for cleft grafting. With a sharp knife make a clean, regular split about one and one-half to two and one-half inches down the small stock, dividing it in two unequal parts. Cut the outer side of the biggest part smooth the same length as the split and sloping inward.

The scion should be of about the same thickness and is split and cut in the same manner as the stock, except that the split and cut outer side will be at the lower end.

A sharp knife only should be used for this operation, and care taken that stock and scion fit exactly into each other.

The whip graft is tied similarly to the cleft graft, with some pliable material, such as yarn or twine. Cover with grafting clay as in cleft grafting. A strip of tinfoil or a band of India rubber may also be wound around the graft in place of the yarn or twine, especially if compelled to graft above ground.

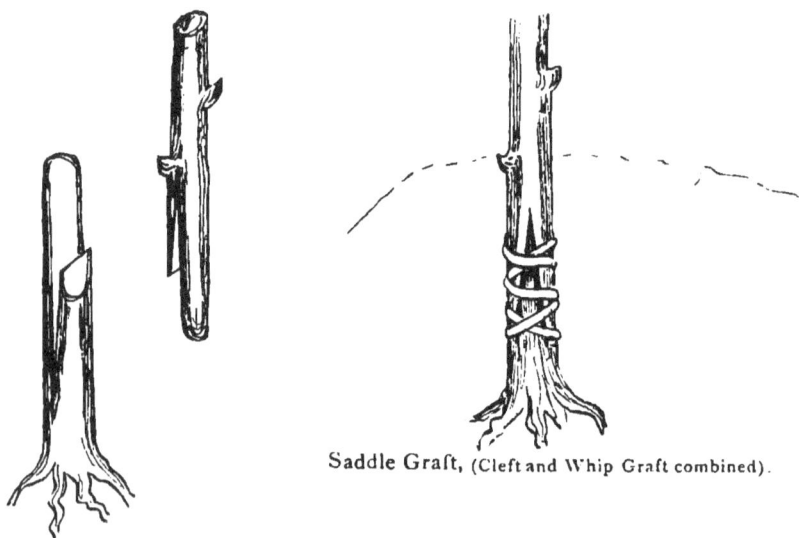

Saddle Graft, (Cleft and Whip Graft combined).

Whip (or Champin) Graft.

There are several other ways of grafting, all of which require more or less professional skill and practical illustration to insure success, and are therefore left out here.

The grafting on layers embodies this advantage, that as there are two ends above the ground, if one fails to grow after being grafted, the stock need not be sacrificed, as is sometimes the case with grafts on cuttings.

Grafts on hard wood varieties are harder to grow than others, but when the operation is performed correctly and at the proper time it generally succeeds well.

The young grafts at first ought to be protected from the noonday sun with some kind of covering. They ought not to be handled roughly nor examined prematurely, as sometimes for as long as six weeks they seem to be dying and then suddenly grow off all right. Wind and weather are often the cause of failure, and not the operation itself.

Grafting may be done on the young vine out of the ground. If this is done in winter, after carefully wrapping them with the tinfoil or strips of India rubber above mentioned, they should be stored in a cellar, packed in sawdust or sand.

GRAFTING ABOVE GROUND.

Grafting above ground may be sometimes advisable and even of greater advantage than the underground methods, especially where a good vine is already established, and it is desired to add new varieties to others on the same stock. It is done when the young shoots have not yet hardened into wood, but have at the base of the leaf the eyes already developed. The operation is performed on one or several young shoots, which are cut off close below an eye. The shoot is then split down to the eye next to the one cut off and the scion inserted after the manner of cleft grafting and wrapped with woolen yarn or other suitable material. Of course the scion should be of a similar young shoot as any harder wood is always more dificult to grow off than any other.

A graft on green wood will develop a shoot of a yard or more in length and generally bring fruit the same season. Whip or other grafts may also be successfully used on the green vine, care being always taken that the different barks fit exactly and snugly.

LOCATION AND SOIL.

Avoid low damp places where water can stagnate about the roots; hillsides, sloping to the south if possible, protected from violent winds, are suitable to grape culture. It may be even necessary to plant some trees for protection from high winds, but care should be taken that the trees are not too near the vine so as to interfere with the roots.

A dry calcareous loam about three feet deep, loose, friable and well drained is good soil for a vineyard. Moderately rich sandy soil is also well suited to most varieties. New soil composed of a mixture of limestone or granite more or less pulverized is preferable to soils that have been long in cultivation.

The *Texas black waxy* where well enough drained has proved to be as favorable to grape culture as any. Fertilizing on starting a vineyard is not only not necessary, but may even be injurious. Only where the soil is of particularly light quality a few bones more or less pulverized, some barnyard manure and leaf-mould, which all ought to have rotted a good while, may be mixed with the dirt, but ought not to be brought in direct contact with the vines.

Too much attention cannot be paid to preparing the soil by a thorough breaking with walking plows or sulkies followed if possible by a subsoil plow in the same furrow. Stumpy or grubby land should be grubbed, wet spots drained and ditched and steep hillsides terraced.

PLANTING.

This may be done in fall or in spring It should not be done during frost or when the ground is wet. Fall planting is preferable, as the dirt during the winter has time to settle around the roots, and the vine would get an early start. If the young vines have not been kept cool enough before planting time and have already sprouted, care must be taken that the roots are then kept moist.

The vines are generally planted in rows six feet apart, and may be checked so that the distance of each vine is six feet each way, which would require 1210 vines to plant one acre [containing 43,560 feet]. Some prefer even larger distances, especially for strong, vigorous growers. Lay off the land in straight rows the required distance and dig the holes for the young vines. It is not considered of advantage to plant cuttings right off. These should always be grown in nursery rows one or two years and then transplanted. Where cuttings are planted two should be put in one place and if both grow off one pulled out afterwards. Even then much replanting may have to be done.

Young rooted vines are the best to plant. These are generally "heeled in" until the right planting time arrives. This is generally done as follows: Where there are many a trench is dug, the vines are placed in it slopingly against the side to where the dirt is thrown, the roots are covered with dirt so that there is a ditch left for the water to drain into and leave the roots comparatively high and dry. The depth of the holes depends much on the soil and weather. In dry and poor soil 12 to 14 inches and in rich land with plenty of moisture 8 inches will be sufficient. The width of the hole to correspond to the size of the vine. The holes should not be dug too long before the actual planting as they may dry out too much.

Every vine ought to be placed so that the top is near the stake and in its natural position as much as possible and the roots shortened or trimmed before with a sharp knife Stakes [cedar] may be set previously in the hole. The dirt worked in with the fingers and pressed to the roots with the foot or otherwise, hilling it up finally. In fall planting the dirt ought to be hilled up especially high so as to prevent water from lodging at the roots.

Planting during frost, also extraordinary late planting should be avoided.

As soon as the vines are planted take a sharp knife, cut all the tops back to only one bud, which will be pretty near the surface of the ground. However strong and nice the buds may look do not allow more than two on the vine. One cane is thus allowed to grow and where there are two buds the weaker one is afterwards pinched off.

CULTIVATING.

During the first spring the young vines must be plowed twice or three times either with a turning plow, double shovel, bull tongue or large sweep. It will not injure in good land in the least to cultivate a row of garden truck or other suitable plants between the rows, providing both the young vines and the middle row are hoed free of all weeds. A cultivator cannot well be used unless it be one that could straddle the row. Therefore, one horse plowing in the vineyard is generally the rule. Of course care must be taken that in plowing the roots near the vine are not cut off.

Do not tie the vines the first season. Some grape growers in the summer break all the shoots off but one and let it grow, others let the young vine alone until fall, when all the leaves have fallen off, when the vine is cut back to a short cane with two or three buds.

In the winter hardly anything is to be done except in case of severe cold weather to cover the vines with dirt or to set posts and make a trellis.

The trellis, which may be made out of wire, slats or laths is generally dispensed with in Texas, and the vines are trained on a single pole or stake and generally kept down in rather a bushy shape. By training vines on a single stake the vineyard can be plowed in several directions, but the fruit and foliage though is also liable to become crowded, which is generally remedied by adding another stake or more.

Where it is intended to grow the grapevine on a wire trellis the posts are set then in between the vines and not close to them. The stakes at either end of the row are braced and one, two or three smooth galvanized wires stretched during the first winter, to which in the next summer the vine is tied.

In some countries in Europe the vine is kept so short that stakes or trellises are dispensed with, but such treatment is not thought practicable for the vigorous American vine.

Early in the next spring the vine should be uncovered. Protection from cold is hardly ever necessary in Texas.

The ground is plowed thoroughly and as close to the young vine as possible without injury to the roots. The plowing is repeated two or three times. A two-pronged hoe (Hexamer's prolonged hoe) is used to loosen the dirt around the vine.

During the summer a cane or shoot will grow from each of the two or three buds left on the vine in the fall. Two of these are tied to the trellis or stake with yarn or other soft, pliable material and (if there are three) the third one is cut off. One or two of these canes may be layered in about June by covering it with dirt about an inch deep, leaving the laterals sticking out of the ground. In the fall such layers will be ready to transplant, making several new young vines. After the leaves have fallen off in the fall in the second season, the laterals or shoots from the two main canes are cut back, leaving of them four or five eyes, and either tied to stakes or wire. This is to concentrate the growth into the two main canes above mentioned.

In the beginning of the third season see that the young canes are all tied well, but not too tight, so as to interfere with the free flow of sap. Hoe and plow as before, somewhat deeper the first and second time than the last.

In this season, from the buds left last fall, young shoots or laterals again will grow and develop into canes, aud each of the canes will probably bear two or three bunches of grapes.

As there is danger of a young vine overbearing itself and thereby injuring its future fruitfuluess, these bunches are thinned out. First, by removing all sickly or weak bunches and otherwise by what is generally, called

SUMMER PRUNING.

This really is done in spring and not in summer, as the name would indicate, when the young shoots or laterals are about six inches long and the small bunches of fruit can be plainly seen.

Commencing at the lower spurs, with the thumb and finger pinch back those buds which are not intended for bearing canes next year, bearing in mind that each part of the vine needs its share of sunlight and air, and that the young wood without such will not ripen perfectly and become vigorous and hardy. Go over each arm of the vine and pinch off every fruit-bearing branch, or lateral, above the last bunch of grapes, and if that is sickly or weak remove it also. Where buds have developed two or three shoots, remove the weakest and leave the strongest. After the pinching as above described, a second and a third pinching becomes necessary.

The buds in the axils of the leaves on the fruit-bearing shoots will each push out a lateral shoot opposite the young bunches. These young shoots are pinched back to the first leaf, so that there will be an additional leaf opposite to each bunch of grapes, increasing in this case the number of leaves to the vine for a proper shade with plenty of ventilation. After this the laterals again will start out until checked by the third pinching, which reduces them again to one leaf.

As stated before, the shoots intended for bearing wood next year are left unchecked, and care must especially be taken that not more than necessary are left.

Some people believe in keeping down the vine more in the shape of a stump sprouting out again, while others believe in "letting alone." But both are in the minority, and a judicious pruning is decidedly essential to permanent success.

Husmann calls attention to the following as objects to be kept in view for summer pruning:

1. To keep the vine within proper bounds, so that it is at all times under the control of the vintner, *without weakening its constitution by robbing it of a great amount of foliage.*

2. *Judicious thinning of the fruit* at a time when no vigor has been expended in its development.

3 *Developing strong, healthy foliage* by forcing the growth of the laterals and having two young, healthy leaves opposite each bunch, which will shade the fruit and serve as conductors of the sap to the fruit.

4. *Growing vigorous canes for next year's fruiting and no more,* thereby making them stronger; as every part of the vine is thus accessible to light and air, the wood will ripen better and more uniformly.

5 *Destruction of noxious insects.* As the vintner has to look over each shoot of the vine, this is done more thoroughly and systematically than by any other process.

FALL OR WINTER PRUNING.

Hardly any rules can be laid down for the pruning that is to be done after the leaves of the vine have fallen off, as different varieties demand different methods. Some varieties will bear best on the branches of the young canes, some on the spurs of a few eyes on old bearing branches, and some will fruit readily upon principal canes. When it is intended to grow fruit on the laterals, these should be shortened to only a few eyes. Those vines bearing best on the spurs of two or three-year-old canes, select for the spurs only strong, well-developed shoots, cut them back to two or three eyes each, cutting out all small or imperfect ones. In all, you may leave from thirty to forty buds, according to the age and strength of the vine. Those bearing upon the principal canes should have the bearing canes cut back to six eyes. The fall pruning will then leave the vine in a more or less curtailed condition.

There are several methods in use for fall pruning and each may be applicable under certain conditions; however, the vintner will have to learn the proper one, by thought practice, observation and experience.

It is an accepted fact in vine culture that the best crops are obtained from the strongest shoots of the previous year's growth; and by starting to prune with a view of securing such shoots, the vintner will be able to determine his subsequent treatment without much risk.

As some vines will bear good crops for a few years even under wrong treatment, it is not advisable to follow any method that may be advocated, unless it has been tried for a number of years and proved successful.

SUBSEQUENT MAGAGEMENT.

After the third year of cultivation the vine may be considered fully established and is cultivated in a similar manner as in the previous years, and careful attention should be paid to the draining of the vineyard, by leaving the water furrow so that it will, if possible, drain any surplus of water in wet weather.

VINES FOR ARBORS OR WALLS.

Only extra strong vines should be used for training for arbors or walls, and these should have rich soil and be cut down one shoot during the first year, or even the second, to make them as strong as possible. In the fall these are cut back to three eyes only, the shoots of which afterwards should be tied to the arbor or wall they are aimed to be trained to. The three canes are cut back in the fall to three buds each, which will finally form three principal branches, each again producing canes the third season. These canes, then, again are cut back until gradually the number of branches is increased. In this manner, in the course of time, a vine can be made to cover a large space and produce an abundance of fruit for an indefinite number of years, if the ground be rich enough, which may be assisted in winter by a top dressing of lime, ashes, bone dust and other suitable material.

Of course the tying will necessarily be in accordance with the design of the vintner, whether for horizontal, round or other spreading of the vine.

MILDEW AND ROT.

These are the two most formidable diseases the grape vine in America is subject to.

Dr. George Engelmann gives the following description:

"The mildew, *peronospora viticola*, appears in frost-like white spots on the under side of leaves, hairy as well as glabrous (smooth) ones, and may generally be observed here in Missouri from the beginning of June, fostered by the sultry and damp or wet weather usual at that season; in the Eastern States it seems to come on later in summer or fall.

Though most common on the leaves, it sometimes also infests the petioles of the leaves, the stems of the bunches and the very young berries. But, even if it does not attack the latter the effect on the leaves alone, which turn brown in spots and are eventually partially or completely killed, destroys the fruit; the berries shriveling from the base, turning light brown without falling off. This is here sometimes termed "brown rot."

* * * * * * * *

"Thus it is seen that the dead mildewed leaves, containing the resting spores, really do preserve the germs for the next season's mildew. These leaves ought to be destroyed by carefully gathering and burning them or by burying them deeply in the ground. The direct destruction of the fungus has been often attempted, and by different means, especially by sulphur sprinkling, but without any marked effect; a dry spell of weather, however, arrests it most effectually for the time being.

* * * * * * * *

" The second great fungus pest of our vineyards is the *Black Rot, Phoma uvicola*. On the berries, but never on the leaves or stems, generally about the time that they are full grown, in July or August, very rarely on half grown berries in June, a light brown spot with a darker central point is observed on the side and not near the stem; this spot spreads, and darker, shining nodules or pustules, plainly visible with the naked eye, begin to protrude above the epidermis*; at last the whole berry shrivels up, turns bluish-black, the pustules roughen the surface; and each one opening at the top emits a whitish worm-like thread which consists of innumerable spores glued together with a mucilaginous coating. In this condition the spores are inert, but rain will dissolve the mucilage and liberate and wash down the spores, or they will fall to the ground with the dead berries. What then becomes of them, whether they enter the soil, or how they propagate the fungus, is as yet unknown. At all events it seems advisable to gather all the affected berries, if such a thing can be done, and destroy them.''

Various methods have been tried to remedy these evils, such as sulphuring, nailing boards over the trellis to keep off heavy dews and others, but all without any real practical result.

For small vineyards, or for a limited number of fine grapes, a covering with paper will undoubtedly be of service. For this purpose common manilla paper bags as used in grocery stores about large enough to fit the bunch when grown, are pulled over the grapes when they are about half grown and are fastened with pins or otherwise. To let the water run through it a small hole is made in the bottom. Of course any other material answering the same purpose, admitting air and partial sunlight, may be used. Covering in this manner, if not an entire preventive against rot or mildew, will at least be of excellent service.

INSECTS.

Besides the Phylloxera, which is almost the only impediment to the successful growing of the delicious vinifera grapes, innumerable other insects both injurious and beneficial to grape culture will invite the vintner's attention.

Of the insect enemies of the grape those living under ground deserve perhaps to be mentioned here, cutworms, attacking the young shoots of the vine and root borers (both giant and others) cutting the roots and following them until the vine dies. This latter is supposed to breed and live in dead oak stumps and for this reason land previously timbered with oak is not considered suitable for a vineyard.

*Skin of the berry.

If any vine is found dying from any unknown cause it is perhaps best to look among the roots for the cause of the death.

For insects depredating above ground—and they are more numerous than any other—a sharp lookout must be kept, and when necessary practical remedies applied, favoring as much as possible the existence of any insect preying upon the depredatory ones.

—

THE CULTIVATION OF THE GRAPE VINE UNDER IRRIGATION.

In that part of the State where the rainfall is considerably regular, the growing of farm and orchard products by any artificial processes of watering will hardly ever be thought of, but in those regions where a drouth of three or six months duration is a never failing recurrence, irrigation is not only advisable, but positively necessary to eventual success.

Where there is an abundance of lasting river water that can be side-tracked into canals or ditches, irrigation becomes an easy task, and money combined with labor will generally be rewarded with good returns, but when water has to be first fetched out of the ground, labor and capital besides require not only more care and forethought, but often a considerable amount of ingenuity.

The use of river water most likely comes nearest the natural way of moistening ground and vegetation than any other, but rain and dew are so far unexcelled towards producing the highest excellence and perfection of a plant Whether the superiority of rain and dew over other ways of watering is due to the ammonia, nitrate of soda or other chemicals that are absorbed in its precipitation, and furnish the plant well dissolved and beneficial nutriment, or whether the action of rain and dew has some other mechanical or chemical advantage, we are unable to state. It is reasonable to suppose, though, that water, to be most efficient towards performing the best results, should be, in substance and contents, as near the condition of rain water at the time of its precipitation as possible. River water being largely the surface drainage of rain water and, besides, continuously exposed to the atmosphere, is therefore best adapted for the purpose of irrigation. And where well or spring water is used, and such should prove to be excessively hard, or otherwise impregnated with mineral matter, a process of softening, either by exposure in the open air or otherwise, may not only be advisable but even necessary.

There are several methods of irrigation—first, *above ground*, by sprinkling, flooding, or in separate furrows, and secondly, *under ground*, in pipes.

SPRINKLING.

This method of irrigation necessitates a confinement of water in pipes and a considerable amount of pressure, and is confined almost exclusively on a small scale to cities, and hardly therefore practiced on a farm. As there is danger of developing mildew and rot on the grape vine by this method of irrigation, due care must be taken that the vine is not kept excessively well supplied with water, but be subjected occasionally to a dry spell of short duration.

All sprinkling during a hot, blazing sun should be avoided, as thereby the foliage can be considerably damaged, and the vine even be killed.

FLOODING.

For this purpose the land is levelled, which necessitates terracing, or step-like division, where the land is on a slope. A small ridge is thrown around each separate little field and the water turned into the highest, and when it is flooded the water, by an opening in the ridge, is turned into the next lower one, and so on successively, until all the fields have been watered. This is repeated generally every three weeks, in a drouth sometimes oftener, hardly ever more, according to the nature of the crops in the field. A complete soaking of the ground is generally deemed sufficient. However advantageous this method may be to other crops, it is not well adapted to an orchard or vineyard, besides an excessive waste of water, and the vintner prefers for the grape vine the

IRRIGATION IN FURROWS.

This method is preferable for cultivated crops, both on account of a greater economy of water supply, and the avoidance of the leveling of the land, which in this method is not absolutely necessary as long as the main ditch is situated higher than all the points of the vineyard to be irrigated.

Where the so-called water furrows of the batch cannot be used, special furrows with a turning or shovel plow must be made, which tap the main ditch and guide the water through the orchard or vineyard in such a manner as to saturate the ground tolerably evenly. Their distance apart may be from three to ten feet. Of course where they are a considerable distance apart the water should be allowed to stand in them for some time, so as to saturate the ground on both sides thoroughly. The water is let in on the highest ground first, then checked in its progress by throwing some dirt in the middle of the furrow; then, when it has been standing some time, it is allowed to proceed further down and checked again.

In this manner a considerable amount of moisture is furnished the roots of the vine without any risk to their foliage. It is best in furrow irrigation to soak the higher ground more than the lower, as water naturally is inclined to seek a 'ower level, and thereby may be distributed more evenly under ground. Where the soil is particularly light or sandy, some simple device made out of lumber may have to be used to check the progress of the water in the furrow, as a light soil on steep ground washes easily. Sometimes a ditch may have to be made by throwing up two ridges, as for instance when a trench in the ground would be too low to carry the water to a certain point. A scraper also may have to be used to remove some surplus dirt. Plows are generally used to best advantage in broken land to open up a ditch, but shovel and spade can hardly be dispensed with.

IRRIGATION IN UNDERGROUND PIPES.

This method is perhaps the most convenient and effective. but at the same time requires the most capital. A level tract of land with some slope is selected. Trenches about eighteen inches deep and from four to eight feet apart are dug, and in them are placed perforated or porous irrigation pipes which extend the whole length or breadth of the field, and the lower end of which may be open and leading into a ditch. They are covered up with dirt and stopped up and the field leveled. The water is turned in at the upper end, either from a ditch or a pipe running at right angles, and the rootlets of the vines or other plants obtain their moisture through the pores or small holes of the underground · pipes. The holes in these pipes must not be large enough for dirt to fall through them, or unduly allow the water to waste. The water in a certain quantity may be allowed to stand in these pipes, or it may be let out after a time into the ditch previously dug at the lower end. In very wet seasons the same pipes, by leaving them open at both ends, may be utilized for drying the land, and to rapidly evaporate surplus moisture.

ARTESIAN WELLS.

From the foregoing it will be seen that irrigation can be accomplished in various ways, and the terrors of drouth shorn from its withering influence—that is, providing you have got the water. When there is an absence of water the solving of the drouth problem, even by the much advocated process of mulching and surface stirring, is as complete a failure as ever.

For in our humble opinion the only cure for hollow-cheeked, red-eyed, fiery-tongued, scorching drouth is water, plenty of it, and water only. Then, how to get it.

The common wells, from which generally the water supply for the use of a farm is obtained, in the middle of a full-fledged drouth show a peculiar tendency which is properly described as "flickering." And even where there is lasting water, the power of lifting it from any depth is generally impracticable, even when adequate, as with a wind mill; but then a wind mill, even, has proved to be lamentably short of wind when its pumping qualities were needed urgently.

Rivers, creeks and springs likewise show a tendency to be become almost invisible, or at least useless for practical purposes, and it becomes plain that if we want water we must get it from above or from below. These are the only two places where it seems to abide with fondness, or sometimes obstinacy. Above, it is in the form of vapor and clouds, and there is apparently plenty of it, but it only comes down when it gets ready, and man, so far, has not been able to accelerate only the slightest precipitation. On the other hand, he has been eminently successful in obtaining water from a greater depth than the common wells, and and it is more than probable that artesian wells—for such we mean—will come nearer solving the drouth problem than anything else. For it may be safely said that there is water almost anywhere, if we only go deep enough. While there have been failures at artesian wells at various depths up to 800 feet, there have been plenty of instances where such failures, by boring deeper—in some cases as much as 1000 feet and more, have ultimately been crowned with success, and the wonderful pressure that great depths seem to possess has become an additional advantage.

This pressure has been in some cases even disastrously great, as in cases of deficient pipes, the soil around the well has been made hopelessly boggy, or in other instances the upward tendency of the water, where the lower end of the pipe did not fit snugly in solid rock or good material, has hollowed and washed out great cavities and incurred the danger of a sinking of the ground around the well, if not a complete collapse. This pressure of the water at great depths, which may be of great advantage to man and also be the cause of complete failure, according to the amount of skill, ingenuity and foresight employed, is by scientists generally accounted for in this way: Water, as melted snow or rain, soaks into the ground, and as there the process of evaporation almost ceases, it retains its volume pretty well undiminished for a long time and finds its way under ground, either in rills, or in streams, which, all leading downward, finally find some kind of a trough, which holds the water imprisoned. Then it is presumed that the passage ways that feed this trough or subterranean reservoir are also filled up with water, and as these are situated higher than the level, the water is, if given an opportunity, inclined to rise in a pipe until it is even with the surface, or highest level of the passage ways. This, of course, may be so, but it is also possible that some other subterranean force may assist in giving this most remarkable pressure—possibly chemical or volcanic influence, though we do not think that the high temperature of purgatory, which probably is quite contiguous to most of the artesian water, should give it the tendency to escape upwards. Be it as it may, artesian water, unlike the surface water collected in common wells, is certainly inclined to rise, and that with considerable force, and in most cases high above the ground. All it asks is to be confined in good, solid piping right from the start-off, and the man who intends to bore for artesian water cannot be too cautious in engaging the longest experience, best machinery, best pipes and greatest care in the undertaking, for of all the unrepairable things, the defective piping or bad workmanship in an artesian well is the most hopeless and disastrous. As it can hardly be previously known what kind of water may be found at a great depth — whether it be saline, briny, calcareous, ferruginous, silicious, sulphurous, carbonated or otherwise minerally impregnated—it will always be advisable to guard against corrosion of the iron pipes by zinc, or other metallic or good paint coating. It will go a long way toward the durability of the pipes and the efficiency of the well.

Water that is brought from a great depth out of the earth generally does not contain the usual amount of atmospheric air that is found in surface water, and it is therefore rightly named "dead."

.   As, for irrigation purposes, the so-called "fresh" or sweet water is desirable, it follows that the usual artesian water, previously to irrigation, should be exposed, in tanks or ditches, to the open air until its "deadness" be somewhat cured, which, with palatable water, will be accomplished in a short time.

Irrigation directly, without collecting water in a tank, from a powerful well may prove practicable on some lands, and on others a deleterious effect may be perceptible. Experience, so far, is very limited, and the practical man will have to exercise his own common sense to prevent a failure.

There are also various ways of softening water for domestic purposes, such as boiling, distilling or adding carbonate of soda, which latter has a tendency to decompose the carbonates and sulphates of lime, magnesia or other salts, and forms an insoluble compound which is slowly precipitated as a fine mud, leaving the water, however, charged with a solution of bi-carbonate and sulphate of soda. On a small scale, and for laundry use, these methods of softening water are perhaps sufficient. For large quantities of water, lime is perhaps the only thing, both on account of its cheapness and comparative ease of access. A milk of unslacked lime is prepared and stirred into the water to be softened, and when it has been stirred some time the water is allowed to clear. The lime will then settle to the bottom of the tank, as precipitated chalk or whiting. The quantity of lime used, of course, varies according to the degrees of hardness of the water.

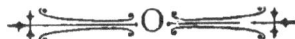

SECOND PART.

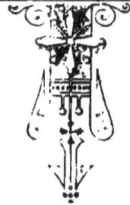

GATHERING THE GRAPE.

The grape vine usually begins to bear in the third year, sometimes also in the second. Grafts on older stocks generally bear the first year.

As the sweetness, aroma and delicious qualities of the grape are only fully developed after perfect maturity, it is self-evident that no grapes, whether for wine or table use, should be gathered until perfectly ripe, which is generally complete when the stems of the berry begin to turn brown and the berry itself has got its real color.

The grape also, unlike any other fruit, does not ripen after picking, so nothing can possibly be gained by any premature gathering, however carefully done, but nature's sweetest essence may be irretrievably lost. Grapes should be gathered when the dew has dried off, and on fair days only. A knife or scissors are best to cut them off with, clipping out at the same time all bad or diseased berries.

It may happen that the first young crop is sometimes destroyed, either by cold weather, drouth or the hands of the vintner. The vine then will, in case of continued favorable weather, bloom again and produce a second crop, which will, if the warm weather last long enough, mature.

If it should happen that the maturing of the grapes is, on account of drouth or other contingencies, delayed, it may be profitable sometimes to wait, as a good rain may mature the crop satisfactorily. But, on the other hand, an excess of moisture may also ruin all that had so far been gained. The vintner's own good judgment in such a case will be the only guide. Overripe grapes, for wine making are preferable to unripe ones.

It will be impressed, possibly, on the vintner's mind at gathering time that a few choice varieties, maturing at or about the same time, are preferable to large varieties ripening at different periods most likely unsuitable to uninterrupted wine-making.

Grapes which are intended to be made into white wine are gathered separate from those for red wine.

Grapes for the market are packed best in shallow boxes or baskets, holding from five to ten pounds. Care should be taken that only good grapes, with the bloom on the berries not rubbed off, are packed, as an inferior article will not establish a good reputation nor command a high price. A sheet of paper is first placed in the box and the grapes packed in it closely, without jamming, leaving the best for the top. Another sheet of paper is placed over the last and the top nailed down.

There are various methods for keeping the grape, but there is none really practicable where any length of time is needed. The best, after all, is wine. Even ice houses are said not to preserve taste and flavor, while they will preserve the good appearance of the grape. For a few months, Fuller recommends a cool room or cellar, with a temperature of 35 or 40 degrees Fahrenheit, with berries all exposed to dry air and then packed in boxes, and occasionally examined and decayed berries removed. Where the cool room or cellar is procurable this is perhaps the best of any.

One peculiar method is the following, by which the grape is preserved on the vine:

About a week before the grape is fully ripe, the bearing cane with its clusters is bent down to the ground and laid into a ditch about one foot deep, made for this purpose, without separating the cane from the vine. The bunches are dusted with flour or sulphur, then covered with soil to protect them from the frost, and so made that the rain will run off.

This is said to be an excellent way to keep the color, freshness and taste of the grape during winter in more northern latitudes, but how it would do in Texas, we are not prepared to say.

WINE.

HOW TO MAKE IT.

Wine, as the fermented juice of the grape is called, is undoubtedly one of the greatest blessings that Divine Providence has placed within easy reach of the human family. For not only does it prove to be healthy food, that the human body may partly subsist on, but in cases of the most emaciated diseases, where life is almost despaired of and medical skill in vain has tried to stop the approach of death, wine has proved to be the only means to allay human sufferings and restore the shattered constitution of the patient to robust health and vigorous life. The most valuable drugs conceal a deadly venom behind their apparent usefulness, while wine in its pure form means nothing but life, health and happiness. When the ravages of time begin to tell on the human frame, circulation is languid and the appetite becomes capricious, according to the best medical authority, wine taken at meals is the cheapest and best restorative. Also in cases of an-aemia (impoverished blood), chlorosis, dyspepsia, nervous exhaustion, sleeplessness, gouty and rheumatic afflictions, wine has not found its equal in health-restoring qualities so far, and it is only an evidence of infinite wisdom that wine was made an essen. tial part of the sacrament, as if to bring more forcibly to human judgment the high virtue contained in the fermented juice of the grape.

Painful indeed is it to observe the ravings of some zealots whose morbid sentimentality and obscured mental vision prevents them from seeing that which is natural. fit, beneficial, glorious and grand.

The readiness and quickness with which the juice of the grape commences fermentation as soon as the skin of the berry is broken and air has access, speaks volumes in favor of fermenting the juice and not letting it spoil or using it with its qualities not properly developed, not to speak of the fact that a special fermenting quality is placed in the grape, that is entirely absent in other vegetable productions, besides the difficulty of keeping the berries for any length of time after maturity

There are other juices of plants or fruits more or less fermented, which are known under the names of wines, but have not the exquisite taste, restorative power, fine bouquet and other qualities peculiar to the fermented juice of the grape.

The grape juice as we find it in the berry and unfermented is called *must* and is chemically speaking composed as follows:

SUGAR, which is by fermentation transformed into alcohol. The less ripe the grapes, the less sugar in the must and alcohol in the wine.

ACIDS, tartaric and tanic, according to the character of the grape; in unripe grapes malic acid is found.

ALBUMEN, a nitrogenous substance, plainly visible in the white scum of the must; some resinous substances, gum coloring matter of the skins, affecting the color, body and taste of the wine.

OTHER INORGANIC MATTER as potash, soda, lime, magnesia, iron, manganese, sulphuric acid, phosphoric acid and chloride. All these substances combined are more or less dissolved in about three or four times their quantity of WATER in the juice of the grape.

While all these constituents are undisturbed in the berry, they immediately undergo a change as soon as the juice is exposed to the open air and begin to form new combinations, and the clear juice at once becomes agitated and turbid. This is fermentation, which is somewhat slower in a lower temperature and quicker or accelerated in warm weather. During fermentation the sugar contained in the juice is formed into alcohol, which again acts on the skin of the berry and separates the coloring matter from it, carbonic acid gas is formed and is constantly bubbling up, and where the juice is in a vessel, pushes upward solid matter set free, so that it forms a thick cover over the liquid. The albumen is oxydized and the whole mass exceedingly agitated and heated. After some time this all subsides and becomes quiet and the undissolved substances settle. *New Wine* is formed. Although some slow fermentation is still going on, it becomes almost clear. The *must* though is by no means entirely converted into wine by this violent fermentation for later on by increased temperature another second similar fermentation will take place, which is caused by the remaining particles of must in the new wine. After this second fermentation the wine will be clear and developed. Much depends on the regular, uninterrupted and complete first fermentation to ensure a thorough settling of the lees and dregs, of which latter the wine ought to be freed as soon as possible. The less undissolved substance in the new wine the better its chances of keeping. However acids, tannin and albumen in small quantities remain after the first fermentation and settle after the second fermentation has subsided, which generally takes place at about blooming time of the vine the next year. After that the wine is still liable to further improvement or sometimes to deterioration according to the treatment it receives. Some wines improve with age and some decidedly do not. Stronger wines are said to keep better than milder ones, and for the purpose of increasing the alcohol, starch sugar is sometimes added to the must in which after the fermentation has taken place it is impossible to detect it.

The must is similarly treated when sour grapes have been mashed and any addition of sugar will necessarily also increase the quality of alcohol.

Wines which are poor in sugar will not do to keep in a cellar for any length of time unless other wine is added from time to time. Those wines that have the requisite amount of sugar or rather alcoholic strength are generally improved by being kept in wooden casks, as water then constantly evaporates through the wood and thereby causes the remaining constituents to be relatively increased or concentrated, making the wine stronger and better flavored. But while wood permits the evaporation of the water of the wine it also allows access of air to the latter so that the wine is liable to become sour and the alcohol be converted into acetic acid. To prevent this more wine is added with a view to keep the component parts in healthy proportion mainly to replace the water thus lost by evaporation. Wines invariably are allowed to remain in wood at least fifteen months, sometimes as long as eight years according to their component parts and strength, after which they are generally bottled. The bottles are kept in horizontal position and all shaking is avoided when handling them, to keep the wine as clear as possible.

Good wine should contain from 10 to 12 per cent. of alcohol, from 1 to 3 per cent. extractive substances, ½ per cent. acids, also bouquet and aroma which is the peculiarity of wine.

As wine scales show specific gravity and not alcoholic strength, it would be advisable to have on hand one of *Occhsels' must scales* at the time of wine making to ascertain the amount of sugar contained in the must which will give afterwards the probable per centage of alcohol in the wine, reckoning 1 per cent. of alcohol for 2 per cent. of sugar. Instructions accompany the instrument. Acidity may also be measured with an acidometer, which instrument can be obtained from any reliable dealer.

Wines are classified according to sugar still contained in them into:

DRY WINES, with all sugar formed into alcohol.

SWEET WINES, which still contain some sugar undecomposed.
According to color into:

RED AND WHITE wines, with various shades in between.

According to the carbonic acid gas contained in the wine into:

STILL AND SPARKLING wines.

The sparkling wine is obtained by part fermentation in bottles, which requires though a certain knowledge and skill, difficult to obtain from books.

VESSELS.

It is self-evident and of the greatest importance that the vessels used, both in gathering the grape and fermenting the juice, are all scrupulously clean, which may be done by plenty of scalding and rinsing with cold water to remove the slightest possibility of fungus growth or spores afterwards affecting the wine. New casks are not fit to be used for holding new wine. They should be alternately treated to hot and cold fresh water, the latter to be replaced daily for several days. A hot lime wash, made of unslacked lime and water, shaken inside the barrel, may be used, after which a washing with cold, fresh water and scalding with hot water ought to follow. Turning the steam of a steam boiler into the barrel will greatly help it.

No cask should be used unless it has been made previously wine-green.

Old casks, as well as new, may be made *wine-green* by pouring into it several gallons of fermenting or boiling hot *new wine*, rolling and turning the cask till every part of it, inside, has been in contact with the hot wine. A pint of pure alcohol or brandy burnt inside of it will also free the wood from the taste which would otherwise taint the wine. Steam, applied long enough, will also remove the woody taste. Old barrels must be treated the same as new. Never use a mouldy or sour cask. Examine all barrels as to tightness before putting wine into them. When perfectly tight, barrels ought to be examined, as foul air may be contained in them, which should be exchanged for pure air before using. All utensils used about the press or otherwise should be perfectly clean.

MASHING, CRUSHING OR TREADING.

As soon as the grapes are gathered they are ready to be mashed; that is, the skins of the berries are bursted. This has been done in various ways. In olden times it was done with the bare feet, then with wooden mashers. Lately mills with notched rollers have been constructed, which may be so adjusted that each berry may be mashed without crushing the kernel, stems or combs of the bunch. The berries are rarely picked from the stems, unless the latter prove to be too acid, or green and damaged. In making red wine, the stems and combs are purposely left with the berries, as they give the red wine peculiar characteristics. The grapes are either mashed in an open vat of about 100 gallons, or, when mashed in a mill, collected in such by having the mill placed above it. The vat is covered soon after being filled.

PRESSING.

This is that part of wine-making whereby the juice, or must, is separated from the hulls and stems, usually called pommace, which at first is left in contact with the must after the mashing. Pressing may be done in various ways. Cider presses may be used, or presses especially made for the purpose. The press ought to be placed so that the wine can easily be run into any vessel, or into a cellar. For a cellar, any storm house, if cool enough in summer, may be used. It should not be hotter than 60 degrees F., or 12 degrees R., in summer, or colder than 50 degrees in winter. Where it is impracticable to have a cellar, a good, cool house, covered thickly, may be built above ground, with special thick walls to keep out heat or cold alike. Too much attention cannot be given to a dry, well ventilated cellar, as by it many of the diseases of the wine, mentioned below, may be prevented.

Cedar tubs, vats or bails are the best to use. All casks should be raised off the ground on supports or layers of timber and should be clear of everything all round so that they can be cleaned and examined.

WHITE WINE.

Any grape, not black or blue, may be made into white wine, and should be mashed soon after picking. Only faulty berries or injurious stems are removed, and the whole either mashed in a tub or vat of 50 or 100 gallons by some soft mode of pressing or by placing the tub or vat under a grape mill and collecting juice and husks in it. The tub or vat is covered as soon as it is filled, with boards or cloth so that fresh air has little access to it and the juice allowed to ferment for 24 or 48 hours, sometimes longer. After that the juice is drawn off from the vat by a spigot hole previously made at the bottom and run into a clean barrel made wine green. The barrel ought not be quite full nor tightly closed, as the fermentation is still going on and the carbonic acid gas, constantly bubbling up, is allowed to escape. Various ways and means have been devised to cover the bunghole and at the same time allow the gas in the barrel to escape. A grape leaf with a bag of sand as weight on top placed over the bung hole is perhaps the best; other ways are cork stoppers with glass tubes leading into some water which allows the gas to escape without admitting air. Care should be taken that everything is kept clean, for if any *must* sticks any where around the barrel it will sour, and if admitted into the wine spoil it also.

The contents of the tub or vat from which the juice has been drawn off are thoroughly pressed in a stout press and the juice collected with the other in the barrel.

When the contents of the latter finally have ceased working or fermenting the barrel is then filled up with similar white wine and tightly closed up with a wooden bung or cork, with a hole bored through the middle and which is stuffed with cotton or any other substance that would admit a little air, but none of the poisonous germs floating in it which are supposed to injure the wine considerably.

As the coloring matter of the red wine is only contained in the skins of the berries it follows that by pressing the juice out of the berry and keeping the hull away from the must a light colored or white wine is obtained. The husks of the black or blue berries thus pressed are then soaked in water to which some sugar is added and after fermenting a few days are given another more thorough pressing whereby red wine of some doubtful quality is produced. Making white wine according to the last described method is at least superfluous as there are plenty grapes wherefrom to make white wine directly, and leaving the black or blue grapes especially for red wine.

RED WINE.

The making of the red wine differs from that of the white wine in this that the fermentation on the husks is protracted much longer, usually from one to two weeks in a vat containing a second and moveable bottom that is designed to hold the husks under the juice and preventing them from rising to the top. Wine, when left too long on the lees or in contact with the crust formed on top will take the disagreeable taste of the husks or stalks. But by the fermentation of one or two weeks the valuable properties of the black or blue grape skin are generally extracted and give the red wine its peculiar characteristic and medical properties.

The black or blue grapes need not be mashed immediately after picking, like the white grapes. The stems might be removed if they are excessively acid. The mashed grapes are put into the open vat, and when full the second bottom, with holes bored through it, is placed in the vat, pressing the husks down so that the pure juice stands a few inches above the second bottom, which ought to be fixed so that it is held down in the juice. The open tub or fermenting vat is more firmly closed than the vat for white wine, as the mush is left in contact with the skins for the time of one or two weeks, it naturally would be exposed to the action of open air, more so than white wine. In closing the vat, therefore, cloth, canvas, boards or other material must be placed so that air is as nearly as possible excluded, while there must be a possibility for the carbonic acid gas bubbling up from the fermenting must to escape through the cloth. An occasional opening of some small aperture will effect this sufficiently if the covering should be perfectly air tight.

After this fermentation, generally towards the end of the second week, the wine is drawn off into barrels, the same as the white wine, and filled up with similar young red wine when no more fermentation is perceptible. The husks are pressed the same as for the white wine. Care should be taken to have the first fermentation of the red wine as complete as possible, as in after fermentation the sweetish sour taste is difficult to remove from the wine. A uniform temperature of about 75 degrees F., or 18 to 20 degrees R., is necessary without any interruption by cold spells between. It may be even necessary to keep up fires when nights should happen to be cool.

TREATMENT OF THE WINE AFTER THE FIRST FERMENTATION.

When the first fermentation, which is the most violent and important one, is completed, both white and red wines are subject to further fermentations.

As cooler weather approaches, usually in about December and January, the wine becomes perfectly clear. It is then drawn off from the sediment that has settled, into a clean wine cask, well prepared with steaming, scalding and wine-greening. By this removal from one cask into another the wine becomes again cloudy, and it will take several months before it clears again. As warm weather approaches, about April, the second fermentation begins. The bungs must be opened and some wine drawn out to make room for the expansion of the liquid and the gas. The grape leaf with a sand bag, or any other appliance keeping the air out of the barrel and at the same time permitting the escape of the carbonic acid gas, is placed over the bung hole. When all the impurities have settled, the wine is drawn off again into a clean, well prepared barrel. The drawing off may be done in various ways. Pumps are successfully used, but care must be taken at all times that the sediment is not disturbed, as the aim is to free the wine from all impurities. Wooden funnels, also, should be used. It may be necessary to draw off the wine as many as six or more times Older wines may be pumped out of one barrel into another by means of hose, but for younger wines this is not advisable. Although air has to be excluded from the wine while in the barrels or vats, to prevent the forming of acetic acid, it is, nevertheless, quite essential to expose the wine to the air while in transit from one barrel to the other. When the object is to make a strong wine, less exposure to the air is advisable. Likewise, wines containing much sugar ought to be kept in closer vessels than those less rich. Older wines would be injured by repeated contact with the air.

As the clearing process is necessarily slow, various means are used to hasten it—such as fining with albumen, isinglass, gum, milk, gypsum, eggs, lime, etc., by filtering, aerating, heating and a few more equally tedious and complicated processes, all which require a practical acquaintance to be successfully used. Lime, if used, will throw down a precipitate of salts of lime, and in case of red wine then will carry down also some of the coloring matter, which may sometimes not be desirable.

In Germany and France, brandy or other alcoholic liquids are thrown over the grape-mash, and in many cases sugar is also added to produce a certain class of wine. But as all those wines and their characteristics are the result of centuries of experience, and as every country produces its own peculiarity of wine, it seems premature to give any hints as to improving wines artificially, when it is hardly known what kind of wine can best be produced in Texas by the natural process. And the natural wine, after all, so far, has not been excelled by any artificial preparation, and it is the peculiarity given by nature, rather than artificial methods, that causes some foreign wines to be so high priced and valuable.

DISEASES OF THE WINE.

Owing to bad manipulation, climatic influences, unclean vessels, damaged or unripe fruit, the wine is subject to deterioration, which is known under the following diseases :

1. TURNING of the wine. This is an affliction of the young wine. The color turns somewhat darker and the wine taste first disappears, and if the disease continues, becomes disagreeable and acid. The wine becomes turbid. The disease is caused by a decomposition of tartar, and seems to occur under special conditions of the weather.

2. ROPINESS of the wine, or mucous fermentation, is a fermentation of vegetable mucous from the sugar of the wine. Wines deficient in tannic acid are liable to this disease.

3. BITTERNESS of the wine, caused by a surplus of sediment left in the wine. The disease is generally cured by drawing off into another clean cask.

4. ACIDIFYING of the wine, where the alcohol is converted into acetic acid, which may be caused by an undue excess of air. The disease can be stopped at the commencement by adding alkaline carbonates, which, though, injure color and taste of the wine.

5. MOULDINESS of the wine is a disease in which mould plants are produced on the surface of the wine, most likely caused by air infected with spores, germs or mould.

Very few directions can be given to cure these diseases, except to remove the cause, where such is known, and to employ an experienced wine cooper, where the quantity of the wine justifies the expense.

For the prevention of them observe the following rules:

1. Use only good, ripe grapes, without the stems where such are unmatured.

2. Clean vessels and utensils.

3. Keep a temperature of about 75 degrees Fahrenheit, or 18 to 20 degrees Reaumur, during fermentation without any interruption.

4. Drawing off in December or January.

5. Drawing off in March or April.

6. Drawing off after second fermentation.

7. Keeping the casks full by refilling them from time to time with similar wine to allow for evaporation.

A process of sulphurizing, to prevent undue fermentation, is applied to sweet wines, which possess an excess of sugar and albuminous matter and little tannic acid, rendering them easily decomposed and liable to mouldiness. It consists of burning inside a barrel a small piece of sulphur—about a thimbleful for a medium sized cask— and pouring in the wine immediately, which then absorbs the sulphurous acid. Care should be taken that the sulphur is pure and no arsenic mixed with it. The one-thousandth part of powdered mustard is used in France for the same purpose for sweet, white wine.

By carefully observing the foregoing rules and suggestions,

the intelligent grape grower will find it an easier matter than is generally supposed to make good, palatable wines, at least for home consumption, and in the course of time he may also successfully compete with vintners of other countries, both American and European, in the general wine market.

I may also here state that so far none of the American varieties, at least this side of the Rocky Mountains, have been suitable for making raisins.

Therefore, wine making will still be the chief object in grape growing. Although the California and foreign wines are considered superior to the wines grown this side of the Rocky Mountains, there is always a fair demand for any fair article, and many a bottle of wine with a high-sounding foreign name labeled on it is drank that was only the product of an unsuspected American vineyard.

Those who wish to engage exclusively in grape growing, we would refer to some more elaborate works and specific writings on the subject, as this small volume is only designed to form a guide for grape culture and wine making for family use.

www.ingramcontent.com/pod-product-compliance
Lightning Source LLC
Chambersburg PA
CBHW021428090426
42739CB00009B/1405